ake a walk down the promenade / look through the windows and through to the back garden

ses / there are outhouses and courtyards that I will never enter / the flo

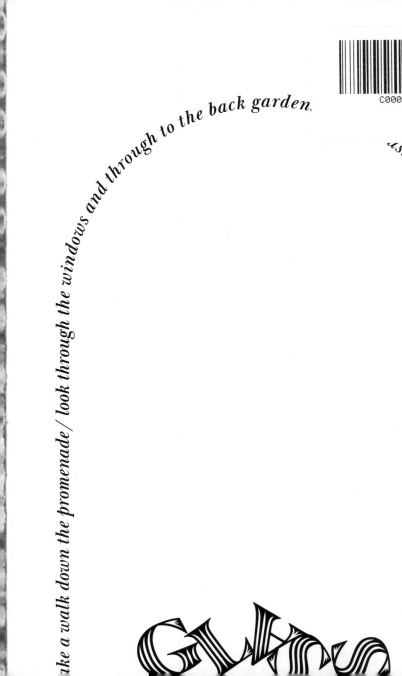

GLASS

Edited by Robin Christian
Design and illustration by Patrick Fisher of Frontwards Design
Photograph by Robin Christian

 Available as an eBook and an audiobook
with audio described cover and transcript.

ISBN 978-1-9160608-8-3
eISBN: 978-1-8384362-3-0

First published in 2021 by Makina Books • makinabooks.com

Printed in the UK by Henry Ling Limited, at the Dorset Press, Dorchester

Glass receives financial assistance from the Arts Council of Ireland

Supported using public funding by
ARTS COUNCIL ENGLAND
LOTTERY FUNDED

Emily Cooper

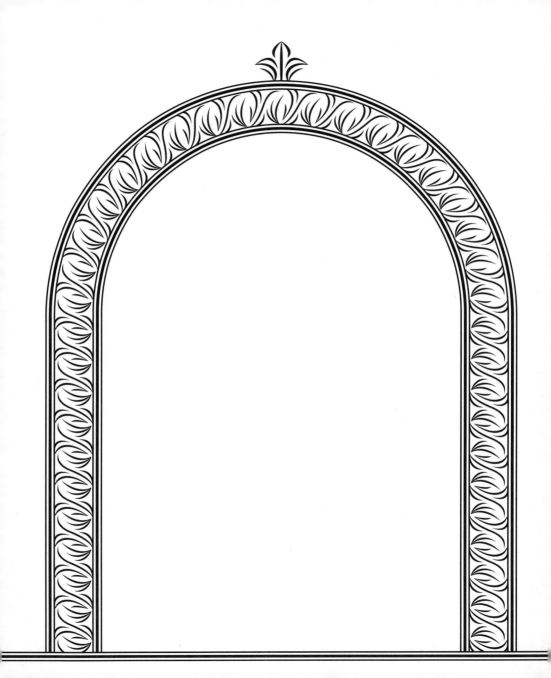

The First Casualty of the Summer

Can a dropped ice cream be a joyful sight?
A slight of thought, akin to roadkill: a dead badger
is still a badger that was once alive.

Can a spark of juvenile pride (the curl tightly
looped to touch the forehead of the whipped pile)
be saved from extinction

once it lies, semi-freddo on the pavement?
Losing shape and form and purpose -
a small death or not one at all.

A fountain pen slices my leg through a bin bag as I move into my new house

They tell you that owning an old house
is more of a guardianship than possession.
Though, it is difficult not to feel the presence
of those who left behind traces;
a cameo under two layers of carpet, a thick seam
of dust between the floorboards, stains
on mattresses and this nib protruding
from a green refuse bag full of letters,
photographs, the covers of address books
collected and left at the door by nephews
and nieces.

Each house has its own smell, when I leave
and come home again after some time
to my mother's house, it smells more like
my grandmother's than when I left.
As if, without the polluting influence
of her half-her children and no husband,
she retreats back up her family tree,
scenting out Donegal and the sea
and a specific soap smell that
drifts out to the front door and the steps.

The slice is doubled, two-stroke.
It does not bleed at first, disappointing
after my bloody scream.
I put the teapot down
beside the vase of forget-me-nots
and touch the wound as it gently swells
out from chalky white to red.

The Misinterpretation of Ripeness

I am often disappointed by oranges.
No amount of hue interpretation
is sufficient to prevent that dry
and yet watery regret that seeps
through each perforated segment.

My face contracts as if hit by
the preferential sourness of taste,
not mood. We share it,
both of us in sudden agreement.

Notions of Sex

I have conversations in my head with my ex about how I don't even want sex anymore/ that I could have it if I wanted it/ that men still look at me/ I see them looking at me/ it's not a competition/ I say/ but if it was I would be winning/ I feel my body born anew without touch/ I can't even imagine being touched/ my skin is ashy with resistance/ my hair is falling out/ I'm hungry all the time but I have no appetite/ I think about the trees I'm planting/ even though I am leaving soon/ will anyone water them?/ I admire the dirt under my fingernails/ the rose thorn scratches up my knees even my sweat smells different/ ferrous/ as if I am rusting/ I find old nails in the soil unbent/ I hammer them into the dry stone wall/ and tie the pear tree to the wall/ it needs support though it is too young for fruit/ I leave orange peels on the window sill and feel embarrassed by my nipples as I drink my coffee/ I think at this point I should talk about masturbation/ but I don't feel like it/ there is a rotten mattress abandoned on my street/ I look to see if anything is hidden in the springs/ there is nothing/ across the wall is the river/ a shag swims past/ later it will dry its wings on a rock/ the tide comes in and goes out faster than I can look out the window/ I miss the turn/ in the woods I feel the trees around me like bodies/ I have read that there is a chemical peace from trees/ I imagine we are sardines together/ me and the firs/ upright/ refusing to lie down on the needly soft ground/ there is a greenhouse on the path/ the glass is all broken/ the pleasure of smashing windows comes back to me/ on building sites as a child/ one after another/ the softness/ the trajectory followed through/ I hold up a hose to a pile of sand/ pretend it's a penis and piss holes like in snow/ a man in shorts waves to me from his bike/ compliments my dog/ no one catcalls anymore/ I was followed once/ in a small town/ I was about twelve/ it got dark but I got away/ you don't forget the feeling of someone watching you round a corner/ is it better not to be watched at all?/ there are new blinds on the windows/ now the locals know whether I'm in or not/ I'm told you're not a local until you get a set of binoculars/ my eyesight has returned/ I forgot my glasses one day and never used them again/ I rub myself with oils/ take tablets to reduce my heat/ my face burns with irritation/ people think I'm angry/ they're only half wrong/ but I've learned to smile in a better way/ let it rise to my eyes/ bare my teeth/ I reel away from hugs/ I don't want to hold hands/ I sit on the steps in the garden/ sunny stones warm me/ I lie down.

her mother was driven to distraction
all up the tiles   the clots filling the drain
pulled off like   rabbit hide
the rows of sharp teeth
fish with less mud in their veins
to die on the deck of her father's boat

Dinner with Raymona

by the blood on the walls
scaffolded by needle bones strips of skin
ripped   over the heads
she would never eat eels again   preferring
fish that have never travelled   from the Sargasso sea
slammed hard against the wooden edge

The Greek Owls

were caged inside a room
that faced onto the owner-of-the-house's
collection of ceramic owls.

        I imagine they were transfixed
        by their simulacra –
        an army of silent thems, not shifting sadly
        from foot to foot.

In another larger cage, there was
a colony of chinchillas. The Owl Room
was specifically nocturnal. The chinchillas
rattled around dimly as we climbed
up the stairs to our small room
with two sets of bunk beds. The master bedroom
had been given over to the owner's
prize Chihuahuas. She herself slept downstairs
in order to be closer to the rest of the dogs
who slept in the kitchen or beside her
in a single bed pushed up against
the dining room wall.

                    She told me she preferred the animals
                    to her own children

In the daytime I mucked out
the herd of Skyrian ponies.
The breeding programme ensured
that the ponies multiplied.
The land area stayed the same,
each foal adding to the daily work.
Around the stables were more cages
with ducks, turkeys and geese
rescued birds of prey
and a twenty-year-old cat
both blind and deaf.
I was shown where
the monkeys used to live.

       We shared our bunkroom with two other cats –
       red and white. Though the owner insisted
       she hated cats.

White cat took to sleeping in my bed.
He was infested with so many fleas
that you could see them jumping
off his scalp and onto Hoppy,
a dog found in a rubbish tip.
So damaged and neglected
they had to cut off half his limbs.
He hopped up and down the stairs
on his vicious back legs,
biting anyone who got in his way.

When I returned home, the barn owls screeched
from the garden, as if one had escaped from the
Owl Room,
followed me back to a certain kind of freedom.

Glass

I buy a slide projector in a charity shop/ another woman is after it/ I avoid eye contact/ lift it up in its cardboard suitcase/ carry it to the counter where an old woman in a reflective vest is waiting to plug it in/ I can hear the other-woman-who-wants-it tutting among the crockery/ we plug it in and it whirrs/ kicks up dust/ *The dust is free!* laughs the woman-in-the-reflective-vest/ *I have plenty at home* I reply with a wink/ the light bulb hasn't switched on/ we press buttons on the top/ eventually find one at the back that works/ I look in the eye of the projector/ it shines back at me/ a miracle.

I google Georgian windows/ try to find out why the front windows mirror the back ones/ creating a tunnel of light/ allowing you to look through the house and out to the back garden/ I keep coming back to Palladio/ our house is simply called Georgian House on official records/ I learn that it was built in 1790/ altered in some way in 1870/ Irish Palladian architecture is unique/ architects came here directly from the continent/ avoided established modes in Britain/ it is marked by an adherence to symmetry/ sometimes balancing on the edges of a Fibonacci curl.

I arrive back at the house with a box full of my father's slides and photographs/ the projector whirs/ I fill one of the wheels with slides/ I'm not sure how to work the mechanism/ I push them into the compartment by hand/ a sideways picture of me on a swing spreads across the attic wall/ I turn the lens to focus the beam/ perhaps I should do this in the dark/ I don't want to wait until night/ there are no curtains up here/ some slides get stuck/ my father on a bridge/ my aunty in a bikini smoking/ an American sign reflected in some water/ I try to gently tease them out/ end up scratching them with my nails.

The builders are in the basement again/ they make a hole in the wall to let light in/ we discuss the future window/ the contractor has his blond child with him/ he throws his red wellies from the great height of his father/ I tell the contractor-with-child that the window needs to be symmetrical/ there should be three vertical panes/ we decide on an opening mechanism/ I arrive to a window with one large pane/ a third cut off/ a small horizontal window that opens at the top/ a 70's bungalow window in a Georgian house.

I rummage through the photographs among the slides/ I have grown tired of inserting them in the machine/ my father was a prolific photographer/ there are photographs of us as babies/ eating yoghurts/ playing with unknown dogs/ there are paper folders of much older portraits/ my grandparent's wedding/ holidays in Kerry in a van/ Flash the whippet/ one of my Grandmother in a green dress/ I recognise it as one I inherited when her house was cleared/ on the back of it is written/ *This was taken at Woodburns House Hotel in March. I made this frock with stole myself it is Jade Green Japanese satin.*

I search the British Museum for a collection of jadeite to compare with Martha Stewart's collection which I have seen on Instagram/ there seems to be everything in the British Museum/ except for jadeite/ I have always loved green/ perhaps for my eyes or perhaps for Ireland/ the Irish for green is *glas*/ on the cabinets in the British Museum are signs/ Do Not Lean on the Glass/ I mingle with the tourists from all around the world/ they seem to congregate in the areas for their own regions/ I try to find Ireland/ all I find are a couple of flimsy torques/ mixed among other objects from Celtic Britain.

Woodburns House Hotel burned down in 1971/ I find a photograph of firemen with hoses wetting a blazing Georgian façade through the windows/ this happened two years before my father's family was burned out of their home and business in North Belfast/ the jade dress must have been among the belongings that survived/ the man jailed for the bombing of the hotel was later charged with fraud involving a string of resorts along the Calabrian coast/ he also blew up a bacon factory.

Every time I go into the basement there is more MDF/ last month they replaced the wooden stairs with sharp edged MDF ones/ it doesn't matter what I say/ it keeps happening/ the contractor-with-child tells me that MDF is an industry standard material/ I explain that this is not an industry standard house/ it is well over 200 years old/ there are no straight walls/ it is no place for MDF/ I catch them making cabinets out of chipboard/ I say nothing.

I take a walk down the promenade/ look through the windows and through to the back gardens of the houses/ there are outhouses and courtyards that I will never enter/ the floorboards lead parallel paths towards this unknown world/ when I get home I will look at the slides again/ force them in front of the bulb/ hold them still as the images glide over the bald patches on the wall where the paintings used to be.

Minotaur By Proxy

The entrance fee was a golden coin I had exchanged for euros
At the bar. A hooded man escorted me to a door that was coin operated.
I asked him repeatedly if I was to insert my coin-from-the-bar
And he was forced to end his silence with an irritated *yes, that coin.*
Inside there was no music, but it felt like there should be music
A specific fairground music, which I endeavoured to play in my head
Accentuating the experience that I had paid for, not handsomely
But with a significant enough amount that I wanted my experience
To be nuanced and to involve an appropriate soundtrack.
I slid down a slide and observed many hazards. Sharp edging
On the metal mesh constructions, low ceilings with no signs.
I could sense other people around me, so I took the most unlikely
Route I could find, round a blind corner towards a dimly lit room.
Here I considered what I wanted from this experience. Was the goal
To stay inside as long as possible, to get my money's worth, or to
Solve the labyrinth and leave with a sense of competitive achievement?

I continued walking around and noting the hazards that I would

Recount to my friends later. A hidden step, a nail protruding

From the frame of a window that was glazed with plexiglass,

A nod to safety consciousness that made me think that

The constructors of the labyrinth had an awareness of safety

Which made their lax attitude even more significant.

Feeling my way along a wall in the dark I felt a gap

And sidestepped through it, considering that its narrowness

Represented a bias towards those of a smaller frame. Unsafe

And sizeist. The gap had a bend in it and transported me into a room

Painted white and lit by a single strip light that was flickering.

No warning sign about seizures. The floor was concrete and empty.

Old Lives

Perhaps if things hadn't turned out
The way they did, and I hadn't left
Eight years before, jumping in beside
Daddy in the car, placing the flower
My boyfriend had given me on the dashboard
Perhaps if the waves had been more violent on
The Irish Sea that crossing, if perhaps
I had taken that as a sign and turned back
Commandeering the wheel
Pushing the captain aside *Get out*
Of my way and sailed back to Scotland
Taken up a job in an allotment
Worked things out with the Greek
Then ditched him later for a tall Scottish
Fella called something like Reuben or
Robin who played in a folk band
Perhaps I would have been happier

Perhaps I wouldn't have gotten that stomach ulcer
And Daddy wouldn't have confused
His cancer for a matching ulcer
They'd just cut it out in time and
We could have gone to the Venice Biennale
That year, like we talked about
Me laughing at his conservative tastes
How he figured craft was of utmost importance
Not this conceptual drivel
Cast a cold eye
On life, On Death
Horsemen pass by!
He'd chant as we walked along canals
Missing the dog at home
That would not jump in a river
And stove its head in the next summer
Perhaps we would all finally learn
How to get along at Christmas
To sit down and eat in peace without
Someone breaking a glass or shouting
About the unfairness of it all
And I'd go back to Glasgow to my empty flat
Get my cat back from the catsitter
Open the window and
Drink a glass of cheap French brandy
To bring in the New Year.

Garlicking

Until I was an adult I always burnt the garlic –
it charcoals so quickly in hot oil.
To temper the heat you must first add onions,
perhaps some carrots and celery. If you choose
to add the garlic first, never look away.
Soon you add the tomatoes.
A quick cooling is civilising. Such as a swim
in a cold sea after you have had a row.
The sea and tears have the same composition,
they taste the same.

Consider wildgarlicking your sourdough.
It will not rise. The antiseptic qualities of the garlic
interfere with the propagation of the yeast.
Their similar wildnesses do nothing to cohere
the two. You must add larger volumes of yeast. Allow it
to bubble to excess. Give longer rising times. Be gentle
but not overly considerate. Use the better basket.

Raw garlic thins the blood.
My Grandfather swore by it. He also recommended
large plastic bottles of 7UP and many hours spent
watching snooker in bed. A garlic clove in the vagina
is a treatment for thrush. Be forewarned of the lingering
metallic taste of garlic in your mouth. Do not be alarmed.
It seems obvious, all these things are connected.

Io At The Table

Io is sitting at the picnic table outside the studio, which means it is after dinnertime. A dog has dug a hole in the flowerbed and is sleeping quietly. I clink two glasses onto the table and the big bottle of brandy thunks its cheapness beside them. We pour the brandy into the glasses. The measures look meagre in the highball glasses, but the emptiness sounds pleasing as we cheers each other. Io is not Greek, but was born on Hydra. In Greek mythology, Io was a mortal woman who became a lover of Zeus. In order to hide her from his wife, Hera, Zeus transformed Io into a heifer. When Hera found out what he had done, she enacted her revenge on Io by sending a gadfly to sting her in perpetuum, causing her to be endlessly restless. Io wandered east towards the Black Sea, through modern-day Turkey, giving the Bosphorus its name, meaning *ox passage*, and eventually arriving in India, a land where cows are sacred. Io-at-the-table tells me this story as a way to explain her attachment to India. A place she has wandered to repeatedly through the years. She now lives in Washington State. She describes the coastline to me. There are whales that swim in the sea there. The dog in the flowerbed rouses herself and comes over to beg for food. We have nothing for her. She is sandy coloured, her breasts are swollen from feeding her puppies. She lies down beside us and licks her prolapsed uterus. She is permanently sore but carries on mothering her pups. It is painful to look at her. Io begins to tell me about a whale in Washington. She was on the news there for days. Her calf had died and she was carrying it on her back – a singular parade of grief – a few hundred metres from land. In the same week a man stole an airplane. A light aircraft. He just walked across the airfield, climbed in and began taxiing down the runway. Once in the air, he put on the headset and air traffic control began to speak to him. Was he a pilot? No, he had taught himself with flight simulators at home in his basement. People who work for air traffic control are valued by their ability to stay calm. It is one of the world's most stressful jobs, combining large-scale co-ordination and crisis control. They continued to speak to the man-in-the-airplane. Io wasn't sure if the person speaking to the man-in-the-airplane was a woman or a man, but the next question they asked was what had happened to him that day? He had had enough, he said, had walked out of the house and just drove. What will you do next? He wasn't sure. They told him there wasn't very much fuel in the aircraft so he would be better to land soon. He was already flying over the sea. He didn't know how to land in water.

The simulator hadn't covered that. He didn't want to land anyway. He suddenly thought of the whale. He had been following the news of her slow transition down the coast. He told traffic control that he wanted to see the whale. Don't you want to land, they asked, what about your wife and children? He said no, he only wanted to see the whale and her daughter. He was done with it all.

Bradycardic Response

They had taken up fishing that summer,
bought a rod from Aldi on a whim.
The two of them would walk
down to the pier and take turns piercing
sweetcorn onto the hook. The pulled-open tin
sitting beside the bottles of beer
they brought with them each day.
'Cheat's bait' it was called,
the fish were attracted to it lazily.
It was bright but lacked the sophistication
of a proper lure. They rarely caught anything,
but that wasn't the point.
He missed the time they spent together that year –
the sun was warmer and burnt less
than it does now. It felt like memory
even as it happened.

One day they were sitting in their usual spot.
He was flicking the sweetcorn into the water,
they hadn't had a tug on the line
and he figured he could trick the fish
into a false sense of security
with free-floating kernels.

A car drove along the pier,
crunching on the sea-blasted concrete.
He said he could remember the sound
so clearly because of the splash.
The two sounds seemed at odds with each other –
long then short.
They jumped up and ran to the edge.
The car floated for a moment on the surface
before it began to sink.
It became lopsided as the driver's-side door opened.
A man clambered out and began treading water,
"Jesus boys, it's freezing in here."

We watched a TV show last night
together in the dark kitchen.
At the end of the episode
a man took his newborn son into a lake
and held him underwater.
The muslin cloth he was wrapped in
floated under the surface for what seemed like minutes.
The father lifted the baby up out of the water and it wailed,
gasping for breath in his face.

Theseus Returns from Crete

After Louis Aragon

The ship the ship the ship
The walls the walls the walls
The stairs the stairs the stairs
The mast the mast the mast
The floors the floors the floors
The doors the doors the doors
The sails the sails the sails
The rugs the rugs the rugs
The spoons the spoons the spoons
The fire the fire the fire
The table the table the table
The crew the crew the crew
The paint the paint the paint
The chairs the chairs the chairs
The plates the plates the plates

The nails the nails the nails
The family the family the family
The books the books the books
The cups the cups the cups
The oars the oars the oars
The cats the cats the cats
The sheets the sheets the sheets
The art the art the art
The babies the babies the babies
The food the food the food
The shoes the shoes the shoes
The windows the windows the windows
The beds the beds the beds
The wine the wine the wine
The knives the knives the knives

The Catsitter

Each morning the male cat comes to lick my fingers
He wants to be close
So close that he lies in my face
His fur infiltrates my nose and mouth

I sleep on as he purrs
All male cats have the same easy love to give

I have to remind myself constantly that this is not my house
Not my bed or my oven, though I am attached to this
Too hot oven and the way it resists opening
Clinging on to its integrity

My dreams are wet. I stand in kitchens that are not my own
But are like my grandmother's without the smell of milk
I watch dark steel waves out the window and consider
How it is always best to live by water

The books are not my books but are like my books
The sections expand and contract, populate themselves
On spines and bleed out into the clippings on the walls
I don't read at all. I just absorb the titles
And the photographs and consider all the jars

It is rude to fill someone else's house with large things
But I want to buy condiments for the house
Condiments are like a compliment –
Adjunct to what is already there

Love is All Consuming

It takes its form in eggs fried in olive oil in the morning
Pancakes piled high and thin, the mistakes left steaming in the bin
It is in the pints of Guinness in the kissing booth of Neachtain's
Creamy heads licked off moustaches and chips afterwards
In Vinnie's. Only hand cut potatoes will do. It takes you out
For dinner and fills the table with plates to be shared, the second
Bottle of wine is always ready, as is the final brandy sipped
To soothe you on the way home, shadow walking together
Along the old stone walls of the hospital

Incredible Things Do Happen

A tiny person at Edith Piaf's grave
turned to my parents
and told them
I am her sister.
Her bones were birdy,
twisted and brittle,
like those left on the number 171,
stripped of flesh, in a small cardboard box.
Her body doubled in on itself
forehead reaching closer
to the concrete of the tomb,
her stick the only thing contriving
to separate the two.
Perhaps it was a lie.
Whoever this woman was,
she's in the Repertoire now,
joining the Kennedys playing baseball
in their garden in Cape Cod,
an immigration inspector who flipped
my mother's passport photo off
with her long acrylic nails
and the young man who presented my aunt
with a huge bunch of flowers in Neary's,
apropos of nothing.